THE *Praying* CHILD

Prayer is the pathway to discipleship that will lead to fulfilling God's purpose for your life.

Norman & Shelley Jones

HOV
PUBLISHING

THE PRAYING CHILD
Prayer is the pathway to discipleship that will lead to fulfilling
God's purpose for your life.

HOV Publishing a division of HOV, LLC.
www.hovpub.com
hopeofvision@gmail.com

Cover Design: Hope of Vision Designs
Editor/Proofread: HOV Publishing

Contact the Author, Norman & Shelley Jones at:
ncjay1@gmail.com

For further information regarding special discounts on bulk purchases, please visit www.hovpub.com

ISBN Paperback: 978-1-942871-96-5
ISBN eBook: 978-1-942871-99-6

10 9 8 7 6 5 4 3 2 1

Printed in the United States of America

Dedication

This book is dedicated to:

Melody & Danyelle

Darlecia & Nyhia Bosfield

Carly & Hunter Govan

Daynean & Dalayna

Dylan & Ashley Augustin

Dashawn Hayes & his siblings

Jabree, Sabria, & Naseem Whitaker

Edith & Jeremiah Gordon

…and all the other children we were blessed

with the opportunity to serve.

Endorsements

Prayer is talking to God and listening to Him - a conversation unlike any other. How amazing is it that the God who rules the universe wants to talk with me! The importance of this conversation daily and frequently ("...pray continually," 1 Thessalonians 5:17) has many benefits. Among them are: 1) we are reminded who God is and who we are; 2) we allow ourselves to be dependent on Him for our needs; 3) we maintain a grateful posture for our blessings, and 4) we can share with Him our concerns in confidence that He hears and cares ("...you are familiar with all of my ways," Psalm 139:3). I can't imagine living life without being connected to God through prayer. I am grateful for how prayer has impacted my daily life and decisions as a Christian husband, father, and leader. I commend Norman and Shelley for writing this book to inspire children to develop their relationship with God through prayer.

John Bryant, CEO
Christ's Home for Children
Warminster PA

––––––––––––

Prayer is important to us as Christians because prayer is communicating with God. As we communicate with Him, we can establish a relationship. We can then draw from His comfort, wisdom, peace, strength, encouragement, and everything else vital for us to live a victorious Christian life.

Keith Echols, Senior Pastor
Word of Faith Christian Center
Aston, PA

Luke 18:1 states, "Then *He* spoke a parable to them, saying men always ought to *Pray* and not lose heart." Prayer is the Christian's clarion call; it is the privilege and the responsibility for His disciples. I am reminded of what John Wesley once said, "It seems that God won't do anything on earth unless man will ask Him." Prayer is our earthly responsibility to bring heaven's order to our daily life. "The heaven, even the heavens, are the *Lord s*; But the earth He has given to the children of men" (Psalm 115:16). As a member of the Body of Christ, the work is done through you. The work of God begins with prayer. We garner success by putting prayer first. Your Father in heaven welcomes your request (1 John 5:14-15).

Bishop Clifton T. Martin, Senior Pastor
Better Way Bible Fellowship
Philadelphia, PA

As Christians, we should develop a prayer life for many reasons. By examining Luke 18:1 (AMPC), we first see that it is a commandment that men ought to always pray. Next, the scripture also tells us not to turn coward, faint, lose heart, or give up. The third reason we pray comes from John 15:7 (AMPC), which tells us that God answers our prayers and anything we ask for according to God's will, will be given to us. Also, prayer gives us the power to cast out demons according to Mark 3:14-15 (AMPC), which states, "…then He appointed twelve, that they might be with Him and that he might send them out to preach. And to have the power to heal sickness and to cast out demons."

Prayer is also how we rebuke the devil; James 4:7 (AMPC) states, "Therefore submit yourselves to God. Resist the devil, and he will flee from you." Luke 18:5 (AMPC) tells us that the widow was persistent in her prayers, meaning she resisted the enemy, and she was granted what she prayed for. As she continued in prayer, she strangled and railed upon the enemy, and her prayers became an intolerable annoyance. So, when we pray, we gain strength, and our prayers cause the enemy to become weak. Prayer is also how we get knowledge and wisdom, according to Ephesians 1:16-17 (AMPC). In closing, and most importantly, prayer is how we communicate with God.

Apostle Devin Park Sr., Senior Pastor
Freedom International Worship Center
Pottstown, PA

The Praying Child

Prayer is the pathway to discipleship that will lead to fulfilling God's purpose for your life.

Norman & Shelley Jones

Foreword

QUESTION – Why is it important to develop a PRAYER Life as a Believer? The word PRAYER (in its different tenses) appears in the Bible 542 times. The types of prayer include Supplication, Intercession, Praying in The Spirit, Consecration, Petition, Praise & Worship, Agreement, and Corporate Prayer. For the disciple, prayer is a way of life. It is a normal conversation with God, a part of your everyday life. Prayer is the greatest power in the world. The disciple who puts in the effort to learn to pray will see the value in their communing with God. Those who do not learn to pray are still living on the natural level of the life that they were redeemed from through the life sacrifice of Jesus. Prayer does not change God, praying aligns you with God's way, and it means you trust Him for the outcome. As you mature in your prayer life, prayer will become a spontaneous expression of your heart to God in faith.

Prayer, in its simplest form, is communication with God. The lack or absence of prayer displays selfishness, not perfecting His love, and ultimately a lack of faith and belief in God's ability. There is no need for it to be complicated. Still, some things should consistently be a part of prayer, including thankfulness, worship, humility, repentance, forgiveness, selflessness, and following God's direction. "...Where your treasure is, there will your heart be also" (Matthew 6:21, KJV). It is evident in Jesus' famous Sermon on the Mount that if prayer is valuable to you, your heart will be involved in it on purpose.

The Bible lists many people that trusted God enough to pray to Him for various reasons. For example, Jesus' prayer life was displayed when He left His disciples to pray and times when he stayed up all night to pray. As He embarked on the most challenging time in His life, He went to the Garden of Gethsemane to pray. It was His connection to God, and it will be yours as well. Prayer will see you through everything that life has to offer. Put prayer first and allow God to change your life and the lives of those around you. God desires your PRAYERS.

Bishop Darin Park, Senior Pastor
Living Water Discipleship Ministries
Norristown, PA

Introduction

Psalm 127:3-5

³ Behold, children are a heritage from the Lord,
The fruit of the womb is a reward.
⁴ Like arrows in the hand of a warrior,
So are the children of one's youth.
⁵ Happy is the man who has his quiver full of them;
They shall not be ashamed, but shall speak with
their enemies in the gate.

Biblical Principles:

Faith – Simple trust in God and in His Word of God followed by the act of simple obedience and response in your daily living (Romans 5:17).

Holiness/Worship – Living with honor to God, so that your words, choices, and actions are the same as God's Word, the Bible (Leviticus 11:44-45). **A hunger and desire for the Word of God** – "Man shall not live by bread alone but by every word that proceeds from the mouth of God" (Joshua 1:8).

Salt and Light of the earth – Salt creates thirst and

light that shines. Be an influence to those around you. (Matthew 5:16)

Fruitful Living – Christianity is about a loving relationship with God, yourself, and others (Galatians 5:22-24).

Disciples – A personal follower of Jesus and His teachings 2 Corinthians 5:18).

Fishers of Men – Jesus commissioned us to go into all the world and make disciples (a personal follower of Jesus and of His teachings). We become fishers of men, regardless of age, by bringing new followers into the Kingdom of God (Matthew 28:18-20, 2 Corinthians 5:18).

Evangelism – The process or act of spreading God's word through the spoken word by preaching or witnessing to individuals.

Purpose and Destiny – Jeremiah 1:5 states, "Before I formed you in the womb, I knew you; before you were born, I sanctified you; I ordained you a prophet to the nations." Before the birth of your child, God called him/her to a place of prominence for Himself. He has trusted you as a parent to guide them to that place He has for them "an expected end" (Jeremiah 29:11). The Bible states those who know their God will do exploits (Daniel 11:32).

Prayer is Communication – How do you get to know someone? You must spend time communicating with them. Communication requires getting their attention by calling them by their name. God has several names found in the Old Testament that will invoke a specific aspect of His personality or abilities on your behalf during prayerful communication. His redemptive names are Jehovah Jireh our Provider (Genesis 22:1-2); Jehovah Tsidkenu our Righteous-ness (Jeremiah 23:56); Jehovah Shalom our Peace (Judges 6:23-24); Jehovah Nissi our Banner of Victory (Exodus 17:14-16), Jehovah Rohi our Shepherd (Psalm 23), Jehovah Shammah, our Ever-present God (Exodus 48:35), Jehovah M'Kaddesh, our Sanctifier (Leviticus 20:7-8), and Jehovah Rophe our Healer (Exodus 15:25-26).

Prayer is the pathway to conquering your soul (the mind, will, and emotions) and displaying humility. It is simply talking to God about the life He has given you, and you asking Him to lead you through it. Your ability to grow and develop in your relationship with the Holy Spirit depends upon prayer. Because the Holy Spirit knows all things, He helps us pray "with groaning that cannot be uttered" (Romans 8:26). Moreover, He helps us comprehend the incomprehensible. As you develop your prayer life, you will be able to tune into or connect with the Holy Spirit, who will not only lead you to pray but lead you as you pray. Prayer is not self-serving. The Lord commands us to pray for others just as Job prayed for his friends because of their foolish behaviors (Job 42:10). We are also encouraged to pray for those in authority that we may live peaceful and quiet lives (1 Timothy 2:2), as well as for enemies (Luke 6:27-28).

Among the different types of prayer are intercession, supplication, consecration, guidance and deliverance, praise, submission, provision, and forgiveness. Be mindful that God's plan for words is that they create. This book is a supplement to the Bible and part of your arsenal as a child of God (Romans 8:14).

As you read and pray with your children, this book will teach the value and necessity of prayer as required by Jesus for His Disciples (Luke 18:1). We suggest using the New King James Version of the Bible because it is easier to read for young children. Please enjoy!

Table of Contents

Chapter 1

Purpose and Destiny

By Apostle Gilbert Coleman Jr.

Unfortunately, millions of children live without any sort of direction from God for their life. Much of this is due to not having an adult who can guide them into their destiny. Yes, I understand that God's intention that every child born should be given the same opportunity in life. However, not every child is afforded an environment where those around them speak positively into their life. Many do not possess the initiative to live anything other than a life of mediocrity. Undoubtedly there will be setbacks, disappointments, and frustrations. Yet, it becomes a matter of perception of these matters as to whether you view them as stepping-stones or hindrances.

At the end of the day, each child must possess an inner tenacity that will not allow them to wilt under intense pressure. They must know that they will fulfill their God-given purpose in their hearts of hearts. Almighty God created each child to make an impact on the earth. This impact is

1

fulfilled because God has given you the necessary tools to solve a particular problem. Many children's greatest frustrations center around not knowing what problem they were sent here to solve. I am convinced that the greatest discovery in life, especially in the tender childhood stage of life, is finding your purpose and fulfilling it to the best of your ability.

Self-Discovery

Never forget that life is what you make it. Your life is in your hands. It can be as great and fulfilling as you decide it should be. Purpose and destiny are calling!

The following scriptures will help you understand that God has purpose and destiny for your life.

Proverbs 28:1
Psalm 139:13-18
Psalm 16:11
Jeremiah 29:11
Ephesians 2;10
Ephesians 3.20

Romans 8:26-33
John 10:10
Deuteronomy 15:5-6
Proverbs 3:5-7
1 Corinthians 3:8-9

Apply this prayer to your life to see God move you in to your purpose and destiny:

"**Father in the Name of Jesus**, I know that everyone, including children, were created with a specific intent and

2

purpose in mind. Help me to hear clearly from you so that I will follow the path that you intended. Give me the mind to lean not to my own understanding, but mold me, form me, and fashion me into who you saw me while I was still in my mother's womb.

The world around me wants to influence me to not hear your voice and to wander astray from that which will fulfill my destiny in the earth. Many generations have strayed away from their calling, but I want nothing more than to leave a spiritual legacy for my children and my children's children.

Father, when I yield to my flesh, please forgive me and lead me back to the pathway of light so that darkness will not consume me. Holy Spirit deliver me from the spirit of doubt and fear. I will go forth boldly and courageously, without fear, defeating anything and everything that would hinder my God-given purpose. I submit and surrender my all to you and trust you so that I will be salt and light in the earth. I am convinced that I am more than a conqueror, and I will see your Kingdom come and your will be done in my life!

Father, my life is in your powerful and capable hands – my only answer to you will always be *Yes, Lord! In Jesus' Name, we pray. Amen.*[1]

Faith In Action

1. Write out Jeremiah 29:11-13.

2. What do these scriptures mean to you?

3. Create a confession from these scriptures:

4. After reading these scriptures, have they changed your perspective (personal view) of God? What are the two most important things for you to seek from Him in prayer?

5. How will they change or guide your prayers with God?

6. What were Jesus' purpose and destiny?

7. What were The Apostle Paul's purpose and destiny?

8. What is the most valuable thing you own?

9. What is the most important thing you will have to do to fulfill your purpose?

---

[1] Apostle Gilbert Coleman Jr, Founder of Transforming the Minds of Men and Pastor Emeritus of Freedom Worldwide Covenant Ministries.

10. Please begin to keep a journal for your dreams, and value your imagination!

Chapter 2

Children in Group/Foster Homes or Adopted Children

Sometimes things happen in your life that you did not expect nor feel that you deserve. You may have been removed from the house you recognize as home. Disappointment, sadness, grief, a sense of loss, rejection, emotional detachment, hurt, frustration, and a range of other emotions may attack your thoughts, mind, and heart. Life may have changed for you drastically, and you may feel that you have no control because you are a child. However, the way you choose to view your circumstance is *your* choice. Please know that there is nothing too hard for God (Jeremiah 32:27).

While things may take you by surprise, it does not surprise God. He is just a prayer away from settling the tremendous turmoil you may be suffering. Please know that I am not saying your feelings are not real; I am actually saying the opposite – they are real! More importantly, God totally understands your emotional state, and He is not upset with you. He wants to teach you how to handle these emotions and give you peace. Isaiah 54:13 says, "All your children shall be taught by the LORD, and great shall be the peace of your children" [that means you when you surrender to Him]. However, He cannot make you surrender to Him (1 Peter 5:7). The choice is yours, and He will never take it back.

You will have to make the hard decision to not allow your future to be controlled by your past. God is bigger than any circumstance that can ever happen in your life. He is the Most High God. The Bible teaches us to be thankful in all things (1 Thessalonians 5:18). As a child, you have God's full permission to approach Him through prayer. Matthew 19:14 states, "Let the little children come to Me, and do not forbid them; for of such is the kingdom of heaven." Prayer is your lifeline to God, and with Him, all things are possible (Matthew19:26).

The following scriptures will help you understand regardless of whose care you are in. You are God's child, and He is waiting to hear your prayer and protect you from your enemies.

Psalm 27:10	Matthew 26:38-39
Ephesians 5:4	Psalm 143:10
James 1:19-20	Galatians 1:4
Romans 5:5	2 Timothy 1:7-8
Romans 12:14	Hebrews 2:15
Romans 8:31, 34, 35, 37, 39	Colossians 2:6

THE *Praying* CHILD

Apply this prayer to your life to experience God's presence and consistent care:

Father, in the Name of Jesus, I am coming to you because you love me, and you said you would ***never*** leave me nor give up on me. The life I am living does not look like the life you want me to have today. God, I need you in a way I never imagined before this happened to me. Please help me to understand your love. I know that I am not alone, but what was normal for me has totally changed, and I feel lost. I really need you. Lord, I need you to help me not lose my fight against unforgiveness, rejection, and bitterness. Holy Spirit teach me how to guard my heart and lead me into the peace of God. I refuse to be a person that is taken hostage by my emotions. I will use the love you put in my heart to love the people you are working through to bring me to the place you desire. Lord, I want to pray for my parents or guardians that are caring for me. I realize that they are hurting now and find themselves in a place where they do not want to be in and might feel like they failed. Heal them, please. Father, I also would like you to bless the lives of my new family (foster/adoptive parents, siblings, and extended family, aunt, uncles, grandparents, cousins, the group home staff, case/social workers, and other support staff in my new journey). Lord grant me stability, so I don't have to experience repeated losses moving to different homes.

God, please open a door for visitation from my natural family so I can see them again. God grant my parents or guardian the grace to do what is needed so that we can be together again. Jesus, I know you had to suffer loss and be away from your Father so that I could have a relationship with Him. Thank you for your prayers for me. They are needed and appreciated. ***In Jesus' Name, Amen.***

Faith in Action

1. Write Psalm 139:14.

2. What word in the English language is defined as "nothing else like this" [Hint first letter is a U]

3. How will you allow this scripture to help shape your self-esteem?

4. Create a confession from this scripture?

5. Locate a scripture that tells you how much God loves you.

6. According to John 14:15, if you love Jesus, what is He expecting from you?

7. How can God use this undesired event in your life?

8. What prominent individual from the Book of Genesis (Chapter 37) in the Old Testament was removed from his family? What was the conclusion of his life?

9. How did the Lord use his life to bless the lives of his family?

Chapter 3

Education

"Train up a child in the way he should go, when he is old, he will not depart from it" (Proverbs 22:6). A key part of your training and development in life will be your education. It is an investment that *you* make that positions *you* to have the future *you* desire. Education creates the ability to think differently. When you think differently, you believe differently and expect different things because you have become different through your thoughts. Education helps you attain the renewed mind that God desires for you (Romans 12:2). Being educated is a lifelong process; learning should be an adventure that stimulates and shapes you. The opportunity to learn comes into your life daily, be on the lookout for it, and take every advantage it offers.

The following scriptures will help you understand the importance of education and knowledge.

Galatians 5:22   Matthew 9:37
Psalm 1:1-3   2 Timothy 2:22-24
Ephesians 4:29   Leviticus 20:26

1 Peter 1:15-16   1 Corinthians 2:16
Ephesians 1:4   Exodus 31:3
Psalm 32:8, 28:5, 1:5, 16:16   Job 28:2
James 1:5, 3:17   Ecclesiastes 7:12, 9:16-18

Apply this prayer to your life so you have the appropriate value of education:

Father, in the name of Jesus, I value the education provided to me for free[2] through the school district; I will not waste it. You have put this system in place as a part of your plan to renew my mind. I will treat my education as a seed. I will sow it into my life with the expectation that it will bring forth a harvest and Godly influence in the future while bringing glory to you. Father, I give my works (efforts and choices) to you, and I trust you because you have given me the mind of Christ and the Holy Spirit, who is my helper. Because of these things, I will excel in school.

I will honor and value my future by prioritizing my education and asking for help if needed. I refuse to allow outside distractions to interfere with my education. This includes video games, social media, peer pressure, sports, television, and movies. School is my place of ministry, and

---

[2] If your education is being paid for by your parents or a scholarship, then you owe them the respect to put the same value on your education and future as they are and more.

that includes ministry to teachers. Being a good student is my faithful service to you. Being **salt and light** will hopefully provide an open door for evangelism. I pray that the government and the educational system would make wise decisions concerning my education.

Lord, I pray that you would protect our schools from attacks on every side that would hurt us. I pray against strife, hatred, payback, unforgiveness in Jesus' name. I break down walls of offense, and with the fruit of my lips, I create an atmosphere of peace and an environment of creativity. I walk in the fruit of the spirit, which includes love, joy, peace, patience, kindness, goodness, faithfulness, gentleness, and self-control.

I pray that my peers are slow to anger and quick to listen. I thank you that they are quick to repent of any wrongdoings. I thank you that my peers have a heart of compassion for one another. I pray that the spirit of wisdom and knowledge will rest upon them, and they are drawn to your word and desire good things that the Lord provides. I thank you for my peers who have a positive attitude toward learning. Place ideas, inventions, and creative ability in them. Lord, I thank you in advance for my peer's success as they pursue a life with you. *In Jesus' name, Amen.*

Faith in Action

1. Why is education important?

2. What part does education play in fulfilling your purpose in God?

3. What role does education play in helping you accomplish your goals?

4. According to Proverbs 8:33, what happens when you hear and value instruction?
   (You become w___)

5.

   According to Proverbs 2:6, where do wisdom, knowledge, and understanding come from? (Hint: _The m____ of G__.)

6. Ultimately who is responsible for your education? (Hint: the answer only has two letters; the first letter is an *m_* .

7. According to Proverbs 1:7, where does wisdom begin?

Chapter 4

Communication/Fellowship with God

Revelations 3:20 states God has come to you and wants to have fellowship. It is of extreme importance that you make time to fellowship (pray), praise, read, and study the Bible. Church attendance, service in ministry, and spending time with other believers help you to grow as a Christian and will help fulfill your God-given ministry. Jesus wants you to be one with Him the same as He, God, and the Holy Spirit are one (John 17:21). Oneness with Him means that the Holy Spirit will be right there when you need Him.

The following scriptures will help you to focus on communing and fellowship with God:

Revelations 3:20
Romans 12:1
Deuteronomy 30:14, 17
Colossians 3:16
John 14:23

1 John 1:3
Psalms 42:1
1 Samuel 3:9
1 Corinthians 1:9
Exodus 33:11-23

***This prayer will guide you in your communion and
fellowship with God:***

Father, in the name of Jesus, I boldly approach your
Throne of Grace. First, I want to thank you for wanting to talk
with me. God, I know that it is your desire that I spend time
opening my heart to you. Father, you said that if I spend time
with you, that you would give me the desires of my heart.

Father, I come expecting you to deposit the things that
you desire for my life into my heart so that I can agree and
align my actions with what you desire for my life. Father, I
know from Jesus the importance of getting away from the
things that come into my life daily and the importance of
spending time hearing your voice.

Holy Spirit, I desire to be led and guided by you into
all truth. I'm not sure what the day holds for me, but I know
that you know everything that will happen, and you will
prepare and help me represent you well. Holy Spirit help me
to speak the ***Word*** into someone's life today. My expectation
is that spending time with you will allow me to become more
like you so I can love you, myself, and others. I know that it
is your desire that I become one with you, just as you are one
with your Son, Jesus.

Today it is my desire that thy kingdom come, and thy will be done in my life. Your word says not to be conformed to the world's way of thinking but transformed by renewing your mind in the word of God (Romans 12:2). By communion and fellowship, I will put your word to practice today, and I will be kept from the evil one. My heart and mind shall not turn away from your commandments and be drawn away to serve other gods [my emotions, bad attitude, selfishness etc.]. Your word is near me – in my mouth and my mind so that I can do what your Word says. I receive your word with gladness in my heart. Spending time in fellowship with You, is just as comfortable as speaking to a friend, my prayer is that I have found favor in your sight that I may know your ways.

Yours is the glory! You only desire goodness for me. I agree with your perfect will for my life today. Lord, let your Word have its home in my heart and mind and dwell richly in me. Holy Spirit [no comma] let my communication and fellowship with you prepare me for the work you have called me to as a laborer in your vineyard today. *In Jesus' name, Amen.*

Faith in Action

1. Write out John 17:21.

19

2. What changes will you make to develop oneness with Jesus?

3. How do you expect your life to change as your relationship with Him grows?

4. Create a confession from this scripture.

5. What changes are you looking forward to as you grow in your communication and fellowship with God?

6. Locate and complete the following scripture in John 14. While speaking to His Disciples, Jesus said, "If you've seen me, you've seen the (Hint: F _ _ _ _ _)."

7. As a Christian, respect, and honor for God are our attitudes, but how are we to approach God in prayer? (Hint: see Proverbs 28:1.)

8. Write your own prayer showing the principles from Proverbs 28:1.

Chapter 5
Obedience to Authority

When you look forward to the life you desire, it is *a good life.* God attaches the good life you desire to honor, esteem, value, and giving high respect to your parents. Ephesians 6:1-3 says that honoring your father and mother comes with the promise of things being well with you. You will not receive God's best without it. As a child of God, you are expected to submit to all governing authorities within the church community and society. This includes church leaders, police, teachers, armed forces, the judicial system, law enforcement, etc. (Romans 13:1). Living for God and being a doer of the Word always puts you on the right side of both spiritual and natural laws.

The following scriptures will help you to focus on respecting authority and obedience:

Deuteronomy 30:15-16
Matthew 5:19
James 1:25
Philippians 4:9
Matthew 7:24-25

Romans 8:28
Job 36:11
Colossians 3:22-23
Ephesians 6:1-3
Leviticus 19:3

Proverbs 20:11   Deuteronomy 5:16

This prayer is an example of how to invite obedience to authority into your life:

Father, in the name of Jesus, I realize that obeying authority means honoring you. Lord, you honored me when Jesus shed His blood for my life to unite us. Father, you asked me, and I agree to honor my mother and father, the first commandment that will result in your promised long life. Just as I choose to honor my parents, I also choose to honor the people they allow to be in authority over my life. This includes my teachers, those who have spiritual authority over me (i.e., elders, ministers, deacons, etc.), and others whom my parents gave authority over me. Law enforcement officers and laws established by local and federal governments (i.e., stop signs, stop lights, and speed limits) are also included.

God, I realize to honor authority is a part of my spiritual worship (Romans 12:1-2) to you. As a disciple of Jesus and a member of the Body of Christ, I realize that it is my goal to pursue the *"well done"* you have for me. However, this cannot happen if I am not honoring and obeying authority. Father, it is your desire that whatever I do in word or deed brings you honor. Ultimately you asked me to let my light so shine before men so that they will see it and glorify you; that will happen when I obey authority. Therefore, God, I commit to honoring the authority you have allowed in my life as a representative of yours. *In Jesus' name, Amen.*

Faith in Action

1. Define what the word honor means?

2. What is the first commandment with a promise attached to it?

3. If you had a friend come over to your house, and that person yelled at and spoke harshly to your parents, how would that make you feel?

4. What would you say to your friend? Would you expect them to apologize to your parents?

5. Do you believe pride is the reason for the times you are disobedient?

6.
7. What scripture have you found it challenging to obey?

8. So, what conversation did you have with yourself the last time you spoke harshly to or about your parents?

9. According to Colossians 2:22-24, when you honor authority, who is being honored in your life?

10. How does honoring authority affect the brightness of your *light* (Matthew 5:16)?

11. Based on Proverbs 20:11, how would you like to be known?

Chapter 6
Holiness

Be holy, for I am holy. Why? So that we represent God well with others. As you read the Bible, see what God does, and then you do it yourself. Study and imitate Him in the same way you do with your parents. (Ephesians 5:1). You should learn your behavior from God. By studying the Bible, you can clearly see God and Jesus' choices. Holiness is living your life following the scriptures and allowing your choices to be directed by the Holy Spirit. God has great expectations for you that will be noticed as you follow Him.

The following scriptures will explain what Holiness is and its benefits:

Ephesians 4:23-24
Hebrews 12:14
1 Peter 2:9
2 Timothy 2:20-22
Galatians 5:22-24
Psalm 1:1-3

Ephesians 4:29-32
Leviticus 20:26
Leviticus 11:44
1 Peter 1:15-16
Ephesians 1:4

This prayer will teach you how to develop the characteristics of holiness:

Father, in the name of Jesus, you asked me to imitate you as a dear child would imitate their father. Father God, I need your help. Holy Spirit, thank you for helping me, thank you for reminding me of the Word of God. Father, thank you that the Word of God has gone down inside me as a seed and is growing and changing me from the inside out. Father, your Word says that I need my mind renewed, and I thank you this is happening through the Word of God. You asked me to bear fruit, and the only way I can do that is to see your Word come to pass in my life. Holy Spirit, teach me how to use the fruit of love, joy, peace, long-suffering, gentleness, goodness, meekness, faithful-ness, and self-control.

Father, I pray that I do not desire to walk in the counsel of the ungodly, but my delight is in the law of the Lord. Father, I thank you for your faith that you have given me and asked me to live by, I believe, and therefore I speak. Holy Spirit, strengthen my body with the Word when I am tempted to do wrong. Father I desire to resemble you in word and deed; therefore, I will be merciful, compassionate, patient, forgiving, and loving. Father, you said that this *world* is not my home and that I should focus my life on you, as did Jesus

26

when He was here storing up treasures in heaven by living with a God-centered focus. Father, I refuse to be corrupted by the things this world offers; these items have no eternal value. You said what profited a man to gain this whole world and lose his soul. I refuse to have my heart swayed by worldly possessions; my goal is to live a life that pleases you,

Father, I yield my tongue to you to pray instead of complaining; I will encourage instead of being demeaning to someone you sent Jesus to die for. Teach me how to be holy, set apart, and be ready to be used by You because your word says be Holy for, I am Holy. Give me the will to flee youthful lust, sins of the flesh, run from temptation, and always do the right thing. Therefore, I have placed my trust in You, because You can do anything except fail, and You desire to do great things through me.

Father, Your Word says Job prayed for his friends. I stand in the gap as an example of how to live a holy life before my friends and their families. Not only I but I prayer other laborers who live holy will come to my friends, minister Jesus to them, and sow seeds of the Word in their hearts that will take root. I decree addictions are broken from their lives and the lives of their parents, which will allow them to live holy while filling their homes with the love, prayer, and peace of God.

Lord, your Word says to pray for the labors, for the harvest is plenty and laborers are few. Turn the heart of parent(s) to You as holy laborers who will come forth in the name of Jesus. As I live on purpose for You, empower me to bring others to you through my life and example of holiness. Reveal to me and stop anything that would hinder me from living holy. Thank You for hearing my prayers. *In Jesus' Name, Amen.*

Faith in Action

1. How does God describe Himself in Leviticus 11:44-45?

2. Define Holiness.

3. As a Christian, what will you use to guide you in Holiness?

4. The Bible sets a standard to be conformed into (Romans 8:29).

5. 1 Corinthians 2:16 guides us into Holiness. It says we should have the (Hint: M____ of C_____).

6. According to Psalm 17:15, what will we see when we awaken?

7. What Jesus' expectations if you refer to Him as Lord (Luke 6:46)?

8. Being transformed begins where, according to Romans 12:1-2?

Chapter 7

Healing

Isaiah 53:5 proclaims, "...by His stripes we are healed," that is, Jesus offered his life as a sacrifice to purchase healing for our physical body. His sacrifice also healed us spiritually, bringing us back into a right relationship with God. John1:1 explains how Jesus was there with God in the beginning, and He was named *The Word*. According to Psalm 107:20, God sent His Word and healed and delivered us from our destruction. Healing from *all our diseases* is a benefit of our relationship with God, according to Psalm 103:3.

The following scriptures demonstrate God's promise of physical and spiritual healing:

Deuteronomy 5:16
Nahum 1:9
John 6:63
Isaiah 55:11
Acts 3:1-9
Matthew 8:17
Exodus 15:26
Deuteronomy 30:19
James 5:13-16

Isaiah 53:4-5
Psalm 30:2
Matthew 4:23
Luke 9:11
Ephesians 6:1-3
Isaiah 54:17
3 John 2
Galatians 3:13
Jeremiah 30:17

This prayer gives you the opportunity to receive healing:

Father, in the name of Jesus, you stated that I am healed by the stripes of Jesus. I thank You for healing my body. I choose to live by faith because I have been justified from sin and sickness by You, Father. Therefore, I refuse to give attention to the symptoms and what appears to my eyesight.

Father, You sent Your Word and healed me and delivered me from my destructions, no weapon formed against me shall prosper. When I feel symptoms that do not align with Your Word, I will continue to trust You and not be discouraged nor distracted. I walk in the victory that Jesus purchased for me through his life, death, burial, and resurrection. Father, Your Word says that the prayer of faith will save the sick; therefore, I approach You with faith and the expectation of Your word coming to pass in my life.

I am healed by the stripes of Jesus; I agree with You, Father, that my healing has come to pass. You will make an utter end to this affliction, and it shall not rise up a second time. I plead the Blood of Jesus over my body because it the temple of the Holy Spirit. I am expecting deliverance from this attack on my body. Sickness came into this world through sin; I have been forgiven my sins through Jesus shed blood, and I refuse to allow this sickness to be in my body. Your Words are spirit, and they are life. As I speak your Words, they shall not return void of power. Your power causes disease to depart. And in Jesus name, and through faith in His name, I am made strong, whom I see and know. Yes, the faith which *comes* through Him has given me this perfect soundness (the state of being in total peace, nothing missing, and nothing broken).

I walk in divine health, I am protected through your Word and Grace therefore, I live a healthy lifestyle. I will have what I say in Jesus' name. I ask you for forgiveness if any of my choices have opened the door to these symptoms. *Healing come forth!* I speak to (whatever part of your body that is being attacked by sickness/disease), and I call it healed. *In the Matchless Name of Jesus, Amen.*

Faith in Action

1. Read Isaiah 53:4-5. What did Jesus suffer to allow Christians to receive healing?

2. Create a confession from this scripture Isaiah 53:4-5.

3. Write out Psalm 107:20.

4. According to Psalm 107, when did God heal us from sickness?

5. How many diseases did He heal?

6. According to John 1:1-5, 14, who is **The Word**?

7. Can you pray for someone to receive healing?

8. Explain what Jesus did in Luke 9:11.

9. What is the promise of Psalm 118:17?

10. What is it that God wants you to declare?

11. Is there a disease that God does not desire to heal?

Chapter 8

Parents

The parental relationship is crucial. Why? Because parents are responsible for you. Also, your relationship with your parents is vital in shaping your life. This connection can significantly affect your relationship with God, either positive or negative. Praying for your parents will help them grow in their desire for the knowledge of God. Your prayers will help you love your parents like God loves them. Your prayers will also allow you to see your parents as God sees them. As parents grow in their relationship with God and the Holy Spirit, it will help you grow in your walk with the Lord and be pleasing to Him. Your parent's Godly example will be reflected in your life.

The following scriptures describe Gods requirements and benefits for a positive parental relationship:

Colossians 3:20   Proverbs 13:1
Luke 18:20   Proverbs 15:5
Deuteronomy 5:16   Proverbs 20:11
Ephesians 6:1-3   Proverbs 23:22, 24-26
Proverbs 6:20   Proverbs 28:7
Proverbs 10:1

This prayer will teach you how to pray for your parents:

Father, in the name of Jesus, Your Word says that You have given me all things that pertain to life and godliness. Out of all the parents in the world, You have given me my mom and dad. Father, I come to You today to pray for my father and my mother. God, You loved them enough to let Jesus die for them. God, I say that my parents will live a faith-filled life that will encourage me to do the same with You. Father, I pray they desire to live a purpose-driven life, one of peace and rest, goodness, abundance, faith, grace, and as co-laborers with You. I pray that they will be holy as You are holy. That they will live in righteousness, seeking first the kingdom, and with the realization that they must care for the life You have given them. I speak the Word that their lives will be used for Your glory that Your Word will be brought to pass in their lives. Father, I pray that they would be as humble as Moses, courageous like Joshua, a man of conviction like David, and the ultimate expression of love and servanthood like Jesus.

God let Your Word dwell in my parent's heart richly, so they can use it to train me up in the way that I should go, and I will not depart far from it. Lord give my parents decrement that they know the state of their children. God, You

36

said my parents are to direct me in this life. Therefore, I decree that my parents are parents of prayer and that their desire is to hear from You to guide me into the life You desire. Because my parents pray, they are watchful over me and lead me away from poor choices. Holy Spirit help my parents to walk in the love of God so that they can love each other well and be a good example for me (and my siblings) so that I (we) will be a good spouse someday. Father help me follow my parent's guidance when I might not understand or agree. I agree to trust them because You placed them in my life with love in their heart for me before I even came to this earth. *In Jesus' Name, Amen.*

Faith in Action

1. Write out Proverbs 6:20.

2. Create a confession from the scripture?

3. According to Proverbs 6:22, what will the commandments do?

4. What time will you set aside to pray for your parents (or guardians)?

5. How will this prayer affect your response to your parent's directions when you disagree?

6. Have you ever asked your parents (or guardian) what they are praying for?

7. Please list their prayers here and refer to them in your prayer time with the Lord.

Chapter 9
Siblings/Family

Loving your siblings and extended family cannot be based on emotions. Romans 5:5 says that the love of God has been deposited into your hearts. Thus, it is available for you to use His love for your sibling(s) and family. God's love always thinks, speaks, believes, and desires the best for others. When you view people through His love, you won't allow their actions to control you. Be conscious of constant complaining, it will contaminate your heart, and you should guard your heart with all diligence because "…out of it flow *all* the issues of life" (Proverbs 4:23).

The devil wants to destroy sibling and family relationships through strife, bitterness, confusion, and unforgiveness. As you mature in the things of God, the devil will attack you he does not want you to love your natural and spiritual brothers and sisters. And if you do that, God will NOT hear your prayers (Matthew 5:24, 6:15). Love thinks the best of others!

The following scriptures demonstrate how to build and maintain family relationships:

Joshua 24:15
Proverbs 4:23
Proverbs 17:17
Proverbs 24:3-4
Matthew 6:14

Matthew 22:39
John 10:10
Ephesian 4:32
Colossians 3:13-15
1 John 4:7, 11

This prayer will express your love for your siblings/family:

Father, in the name of Jesus, I claim my siblings and my entire family as members of the Body of Christ who have received Jesus as their Lord and Savior. As for me and my house, we will serve the Lord. Because we choose to live by and put the Word of God in practice in our lives, our house will be established. It will be filled with your precious promises of peace, love, joy, contentment, and other Godly pleasures. I commit my family to You. God, I ask that You keep them safe, I say that they are operating in the sound mind You have provided for them, and that safe thinking leads them in Your will.

Father, I thank You for blessing my family with every spiritual blessing that causes them to live in peace and prosperity. Father, I say that we will use the love that You have shed abroad in our hearts to love each other in times of disagreement. My family will not be servants to their emotions. We will forgive each other when necessary. Father, I say that my siblings and family will prosper because our soul is prospering.

We choose to live in harmony with one another. With Jesus as our example, we will serve one another in love. My family lives in the healing that was purchased for them by the stripes of Jesus. With God's love in our family, we will be responsible, reliable, trustworthy, loyal, and accountable to one another. All men will know that we are Your disciples because of our love for one another. Father, I thank You for the grace You give my family because they love You. *In Jesus' Name, Amen.*

Faith in Action

1. Write Ephesians 4:32.

2. Why is forgiveness important?

3. Define the word *tenderhearted*.

4. List a time when you were tenderhearted toward your sibling.

5. The next time, what will you do differently?

6. What has God shared with you out of the kindness of His heart? (Hint: F_ _ _ g _ _ _ _ _s.)

7. When you share, what does this display? (Hint: being t_ _ _ _ _h_ _ _ _ _ _d.)

8. Are you good at sharing with your sibling(s) or friends?

9. How can you improve your sharing with your sibling(s) or friends?

Chapter 10

Managing Your Emotions

Your emotions are a great servant; however, they can also turn you into their slave! Being emotionally driven is characteristic of babies who lack the verbal ability and mental maturity to express themselves properly. When the sin of pride rears its ugly head, it causes an emotional response. When someone does something we don't like or agree with, what we are saying is, "how could you treat me like that?" or "how could you say that to me?" That is our *ego* exposing itself. Be mindful *E.G.O.* stands for Edging God Out! Where is your compassion or empathy? Are you unwilling to see or even show interest in the other person's side? Ask yourself, "What has happened to them?" Did you ever think, "Why do they believe their actions are normal?" These questions should prompt you to realize their response is inappropriate for a reason!

As a child of God, you are required to respond to God with love and humility. Even when you have challenging times in your life, the requirement does not change. Now you know why you have to develop a prayer life. God has provided many different strategies to help us when we are attacked by our emotions: bear one another's burdens (Galatians 6:2), mercy and truth (Proverbs 3:3), patience and long-suffering (Galatians 5:22-24), and praying for your enemies (Luke 6:35). When it comes down to it ask yourself this, will you *allow* a choice someone else made (that you do not agree with) to cause you to make a choice that GOD does not agree with?

The following scriptures will provide guidance for emotion management:

Ecclesiastes 5:2
John 14:26
Romans 12:1
1 Corinthians 2:16
2 Corinthians 10:5

Galatians 5:22-24
Philippians 4:8
Colossians 3:12-14
James 1:8
2 Peter 1:5-7

This prayer will help you submit your mind and emotions to God:

Father, in the Name of Jesus, I ask you to help me control my thoughts. You said, cast down every imagination that exalts itself against the knowledge of God, bringing into captivity every thought to the obedience of Christ. I will make a commitment to renew my mind with the word of God daily and speak it as well. Holy Spirit help me regulate my emotions and thoughts to think and respond like you. I will pursue peace.

Your word says that I have the mind of Christ. Therefore, I think about things that are true, just, pure, lovely, and are of a good report. Holy Spirit, you are my helper; therefore, help me keep my mind firm and sure, and bring back things to my remembrance. Guide me into all truth through your word. Help me not to lean to my own understanding, but in all my ways acknowledge you, then you will direct my paths. Holy Spirit help me not to waver but be single-minded in all my ways of thinking. Because I live by the Word of God, I will not stumble nor fall. Father, your word lights the path that I am taking, so my steps are sure. *In Jesus' Name, Amen.*

Faith in Action

1. Emotions can be good servants, but *poor masters!* Your emotions often are an attack from something unpleasant or a disappointment. What are the skills you will need to handle negative emotions?

2. Write out Galatians 5:22-24.

3. According to Philippians 4:5, what can you do to allow God to help you with disappointment and negative emotions?

4. Read Proverbs 25:28. How can this verse help you to rule over your emotions?

5. Read 2 Peter 1:5-8. Which of these characteristics found in this scripture will guide you through challenging times (when your emotions can lead in the wrong direction) so you can respond the way God would prefer?

6. Read 1 Peter 5:7. Are you holding on to something that you should release? Now, re-write this verse using your own words.

Chapter 11
Self-Esteem

Having healthy self-esteem is important; at the same time possessing humility is vital because it will help you in your relationships. It will keep you balanced and keep you comfortable in your current situation. Developing self-esteem will keep you from being envious, jealous, and/or covetousness. The way to accomplish this is to see yourself as valuable enough for Jesus to die for. If someone asked you who is greater, Superman or Clark Kent? Most would say Superman. Not so, Clark Kent displays his self-esteem by going into the phone booth and changing into Superman. He does not try to take over so that people will honor him; he realizes his place and is comfortable. What you place a high value on can cause you to belittle yourself if you have not achieved it *yet*.

You will be rewarded at the appointed time, like when Samuel came to find David (1 Samuel 16:7). Why is a $5 bill less valuable than a $20? Same size and quality of paper, the same amount of ink, same labor? Well? A ***decision***! You must decide that your value comes from the constant of God's Love, the Blood of Jesus, and His life sacrifice for you! Do not allow things to create your self-esteem (clothes, toys, phones, etc.). Depression in youth has reached an all-time high. Not having the appropriate value for yourself will open the door to the enemy of depression, which far too often leads to substance abuse (that could begin with prescription drugs).

Think about this – would you pay to work for someone? But why are you willing to pay to advertise someone's designer clothes, shoes, phones, toys, and accessories for them? Are you looking for value and recognition from others? Consider how much companies pay for television, magazines, radio, and the internet for advertising. Remember that God has already decided you are valuable enough to have His Son Jesus die for you. That alone makes you special and valuable.

The following scriptures will:

Psalm 37:1-5,146:5
1 Timothy 6:6
Philippians 4:11
Proverbs 23:17-18

Hebrews 13:5
Jeremiah 17:7
Psalm 139:13-14
2 Corinthians 1:2

This prayer will allow the development of your self-esteem Biblically:

Father, in the Name of Jesus, I choose to trust in and receive self-confidence from you. The Word of God says You have set me on high (Psalm 91:14). You have put me in a place of high esteem and value. Because I commit myself to You and put my hope in You, I have received the blessing from You and it will bring me in the presence of great men and women. I refuse to look outside of my relationship with You to search for my value. Father, your love for me and the blood Jesus shed for me has given me the greatest thing that I could have – *a presence with You.* Righteousness allows me to pray to You; nothing has more value than this. Father, you said I could cast all my cares on you. Anything that is bothering me, I can talk with You about it. Lord, sometimes I look at people, places, and things and allow them to become more valuable than who You have created me to be, please forgive me.

Lord, you have a plan for me; you are working on, in and through me to complete the plan for my life like you promised. Your thoughts for me are good and for an expected end. Father, your purpose for me is the most valuable thing I own. I will not allow anything to get in front of it or allow me

49

to view it as less valuable. Godliness with contentment yields gain and there is no end to my expectation of You. Father, all that You have promised me keeps me content and excited. You are faithful. I choose humility so that you can view me as the greatest in the kingdom of heaven. You are working all things for my good. Thank you, Father, for more grace. *In Jesus' Name, Amen.*

Faith in Action

1. Throughout the Bible, God has empowered you with His Grace, along with allowing the Holy Spirit to guide you. Please fill in the blank about how God refers to it in the following scriptures:

    *   Joshua 1:9 (Hint: good C_____e)
    *   Psalm 27:3 (Hint: C__f____t)
    *   Psalm 139 (Hint: three words – F___f___y and W__d_____y M__e.)

2. In Hebrews 13:5, God displays His value for you by promising that He will never: (complete sentence).

3. John 3:16 teaches us that we are valuable enough to Jesus that He did what? (Hint: D_ _ on the C_ _ _ _.)

4. How much of your time, talent, money, gifts, and attention have you given to things that have no value to you?

5. Now consider Philippians 1:6 and see how much God is committed to your success.

Chapter 12

Trouble in The Family

The devil comes to kill, steal, and destroy (John 10:10). This was demonstrated in the Garden of Eden (Genesis 3:1-7) where the original family experienced trouble. Adam did not provide the proper support, encouragement, or empowerment for Eve. This left her open to the lies of the enemy. After Adam joined Eve in disobeying God's will, he blamed her for eating the fruit Eve offered to him.

Consequently, this brought trouble to the family of God which included God, this was the original family disagreement. Adam and Eve's disobedience led to the choices that were made by God to repair what had been damaged by Adam and Eve. The first thing God did was to display His Love. He provided everything necessary for their forgiveness and restoration. He made a covenant with Adam and Eve, then welcomed them back into a relationship with Him. Next, and sadly enough, Adam and Eve's sons experienced conflict as well.

Cain became jealous and envious of Abel because God rejected his inferior offering. In contrast, Abel offered the best he had, which God accepted. An argument ensued, which led to Cain killing his brother Abel violating God's sixth commandment (Exodus 20:13).

It is practically impossible for families not to experience minor to extreme troubles. Among the most common issues are divorce, separation, death, prolonged sickness, physical fighting, spousal abuse, substance abuse, and judicial system issues, including incarceration. To bring restoration to your family, you will have to do the thing God did, that is provide the pathway through prayer. Sometimes a simple phone call or visit is enough to repair what has been broken. Love conquers *all*!

The following scriptures will show the importance of having the right attitude for family unity:

John10:10
Genesis 50:15,17, 20-21
Proverbs17:13
Genesis 4:1-12
Romans 12:9-10,18
Ephesians 4:26
Philippians 2:4

Psalm 51:17
Mark 3:25
Proverbs 16:24
Proverbs 17:1
1 Corinthians 13:4-8
Matthew 6:14, 18:21-22

This prayer helps to strengthen your family in troubling times:

Father in the Name of Jesus, I have chosen to spend time with you, worshiping and praising you because my confidence is in You. I put my trust in You because You covered me and promised You would never leave me! I turn to You, Father because you are my strength. Lord, I expect You to rescue and protect my family and me during this challenging time. Holy Spirit, I ask You to cover us. I trust in God's faithful promises, which are my armor and protection. I refuse to be afraid of what comes against me, I choose to keep my eyes on your promises. Greater is He that is in me than the things that are coming against me. Lord, You are the glory and lifter of my head when discouragement tries to keep me down.

I have perfect peace and confidence in Christ because He loved me enough to die for me. Lord, You promised to comfort me and encourage me in the time of trouble; I receive Your peace today. Even though I may be pressed on every side, I refuse to give up on trusting you. Your love for me, Father, will conquer anything that could ever come against me. I speak to discouragement now and tell it to ***get away from me now***! I have the strength for all things in Christ Jesus because the Holy Spirit equips me for success. My complete and total belief in God's love for me keeps me stable and standing in faith. ***In Jesus' Name, Amen.***

Faith in Action

1. As a Christian, what is the number one characteristic you will have to develop? (Hint: F _ _ g _ _ _ n _ _ s).

2. Write out John 10:10.

3. What does the enemy come to do?

4. What did Jesus come to bring?

5. What is the promise Jesus makes us in John 16:33 when we have difficult times?

6. According to 1 John 5:5, what is the benefit of accepting Jesus as Lord and Savior?

7. How do you feel now since you have this information?

8. Create a confession from Revelation 12:11. By the blood of Jesus, my family is an (Hint: O _ _ _ c_ _ _ r).

Chapter 13

Finances

John 3:16 is arguably one of the most popular scriptures in the Bible, it reveals God's most astounding attribute. It states, "For God so loved the world that He gave His only begotten Son, that whoever believes in Him should not perish but have everlasting life." The keywords are, "*He gives!*" Even in the most challenging times, according to Genesis 22:13, God shows us when you have to make a decision that makes no sense He will provide for you through obedience. With the heart man believes, not with their head.

God's financial plan is tithing, offering, alms (giving money for Godly causes), helping to fund the Gospel of the Kingdom and to fulfill His purpose for your life. Money is a tool and a necessity on the earth. Money is used to obtain something of value. What and where you decide to sow, spend, or invest the money God has provided for you displays the value you have placed on something or someone.

Being a good money manager (steward) will determine how much money God can trust you with (Matthew

25:14-30). Spending money on toys, video games, clothes, sneakers, and other material possessions due to peer pressure or to create self-esteem will lead to poor spending habits and a lack of investment in things more important. Learning simple financial planning, like saving money you receive from an allowance or any other way the Lord might bless you with is a wise choice. This will help you to become a good steward of God's money, then *He* can trust you with an abundant increase of money!

The following scriptures provide an understanding of the importance of money and how to manage money:

Psalm 37:25

Malachi 3:10

John 3:16

Matthew 6:24-34

Jeremiah 1:12

1 Peter 5:7

Proverbs 10:22

Psalms 34:1

1 John 1:9

Romans 10:10

Philippians 4:6

This prayer will help transform you into a good financial steward:

Father, in the name of Jesus, I thank You for all provisions! God, You are a giver, and your Word says that You would not see the righteous forsaken, nor his seed begging for bread. Today I come to You Father and express the need for more finances in my life, to take are of_____. You said that if I seek and pursue God's kingdom and all its righteousness, You will add all things to me. The Bible says that You watch over your Word to perform it, so Father, I thank you for performing your Word in my life today. Your Word says that you watch over the birds and provide for them; you said that I am more valuable than them; therefore, I know You will provide for me.

I cast this care of _____ to You for my financial needs. I will not worry or be anxious, but I will trust You. You know what I need, and I thank You for the financial provision to take care of these things. Lord, I believe your blessing makes me rich and adds no sorrow with it. I thank You for all provisions, both spiritual and natural. Lord, I have received from You the most valuable thing that I could ever possess – forgiveness for my sins and your salvation. Therefore, I believe I receive my financial needs. *In the Name of Jesus, Amen.*

Faith in Action

1. Read and study (then answer questions 2-6) Malachi 3:8-10.

2. What does God accuse men of doing?

3. In what area?

4. What will happen as a result of this poor choice?

5. What does God instruct you to do with your finances?

6. If you follow God's instructions, what does He promise to do?

7. How do people benefit from the finances that are given to the church?

8. Our finances represent the return on the effort we put out. Whether it is chores at home, money for your report card, working, or even as a gift (kind gesture, birthday, or holiday), they all come as a response to God. Therefore, honor God by giving some to Him so the Gospel message can be shared with others through the church. Has this helped you see the value of money differently? Please explain.

Chapter 14

Peace and Protection in Troubled Times

Psalm 30:5 states, "Weeping may endure for a night, but joy comes in the morning." Your night could physically be one night, or it could be a period in your life, whether that be a week, a month, or longer. The truth is we would like not to have any trouble in our lives because we have accepted The Lord Jesus as our personal Savior. However, He told us there would be trouble in this life (John 16:33). God expects us to *live by faith*, that is, to believe, trust, and rely on His Word and be obedient to the Holy Spirit. When we do, we can see Him amid our troubles, including divorce/or separation, bullying, loss of a loved one, a job, struggling with school grades, relationships, etc.

You are the apple of God's eye. He is in the business of saving His children (Psalm17:7-8). He is our deliverer and fortress in Him do we trust (Psalm 91:2). He promised He would never leave nor forsake you. God does *not* bring you trouble, the devil does! The Bible states the devil comes into your life to kill, steal, and destroy (John 10:10). The devil wants to influence you to make choices that may physically kill you, steal your vision and dreams, and destroy your God-given purpose. God's will is to lead you to a place of peacefulness. In John 14:27, God tells us to fear not because He gives us peace – not the kind the world gives. Therefore, our hearts will not be troubled because of Jesus' peace.

The following scriptures will help you find peace and protection in times of trouble:

Philippians 4:7
Psalm 37:37, 34:14, 50:15
Psalm 23
Psalm 91
1 Corinthians 10:13
2 Thessalonians 3:16

Numbers 6:26
1 John 4:4
Hebrews 13:5
Deuteronomy 31:8
Joshua 1:5
Romans 8:31

This prayer will help you find peace and protection in times of trouble:

Father, in the Name of Jesus, You said in Your Word that You would make an everlasting covenant of peace with me. Father, You said to call on You in the day of trouble. I need Your help! Lord, today the peace You said You have given me is under attack by_____. I come to You because I need Your peace to rule in my heart right now.

Father, Your Word says that the days that we live in are evil and that the enemy of my soul is using people, places, and things to attack me. I am coming to You, Father, in expectation of Your Word. My desire is to glorify You in my body. I will not give more attention to what is coming against me on the outside. I will give my attention to the peace that I have received from you, which is inside.

Holy Spirit, You are my helper. I agree with You that my faith has saved me, and I can go in peace. I will let the peace of God rule in my heart. That is what You have called me to, Father. Greater is He that is within me than the things of this world coming against me. I believe and trust in Your love Father. You said that You would never leave me nor forsake me, and in the time of trouble, You would make a way of escape for me when I am tempted by the devil to do wrong. I thank You for that way of escape. Father, Your Word says that goodness and mercy will follow me all the days of my life. I yield right now to goodness and mercy. Father I pray for_____, that he/she/they would depart from evil, do good, seek peace, and pursue it for that is Your will for_____. God, thank you for protection from _____, which seeks to harm me, but it cannot succeed because You are my God. Holy Spirit open my spiritual eyes during this attack. Show me if my actions have brought any of the negative consequences of suffering. If I have opened the door to this attack, I repent! Please forgive me. Right now, I receive the peace of God that passes all understanding that peace will keep my heart and my mind through *Christ Jesus, Amen.*

Faith in Action

1. Read James 1:2-8. What attitude will you display during difficult times?
2. According to Nehemiah 8:10, what will joy do for you in troubled times?
3. Read Hebrews 10:35. Write it in your own words.
4. What does the word *cast* mean in Hebrews 10:35?
5. Read 2 Corinthians 12:8-10. According to God, when is strength at its best?
6. Read Roman 8:38-39. The trouble that you experience right now cannot.
7. What did Jesus shed that will give you victory?
8. Have you prayed in a time of trouble for the person who created the issues (if applicable)?

Chapter 15

Healthy Lifestyle

1 Corinthians 6:19-20 teaches us that we have been rescued from the devil as believers. As born-again believers, our lives have been bought and paid for with the sacrifice and blood of Jesus. Therefore, we do not belong to ourselves. Now think about how you would want someone to take care of something they borrowed from you. When making choices for your life and body, just remember your decisions' cost was Jesus' shed blood. Take a moment to think about *all* the things you do with your body: eating, drinking, adequate sleep, drugs (prescription and illegal), cigarettes, alcohol, sex, and of course, exercising. Not taking proper care of the body that Jesus died for will directly affect your ability to fulfill God's purpose for your life.

Consider this, you were made by Him (Colossians 1:16). He redeemed you by the shedding of His precious blood. As a result, what you do with the body is very important to Jesus. Therefore, you are not of your own, and He should have the final say in the choices you make. "Trust in the Lord with all your heart and lean not to your own understanding, in **all** your ways acknowledge Him, and He will direct your paths" (Proverbs 3:5-6).

You are born with muscle and bone, along with some fat. As your bones and muscle grow and develop, you will have to lift weights if you desire to enhance your tone and strength. Yes, you will have to on purpose lift more weight than you can currently handle to enlarge and define your muscles. Discomfort or pain will play a part in achieving the appearance you desire for your body. You will have to make conscious and purposeful choices to care for the body for which Jesus died. Exercise, diet, and sleeping will directly affect the length of time you live.

Consider how you would feel if someone borrowed something from you but then did things with it that you disagreed with. For example, if your friend was careless with your expensive iPad or iPhone, or they purposely walked through mud in your favorite sneakers they borrowed. Their actions reflect they do not take care of nor value what belongs to you. Jesus feels the same about you. You are not your own; the Holy Spirit lives within you (1 Corinthians 6:19). You were bought with a price. Jesus redeemed (rescued) you.

THE *Praying* CHILD

The following scriptures will help you understand how God views your health:

1 Corinthians 6:19-20   1 Peter 5:8-9
1 Corinthians 7:23   3 John 2
Exodus 23:25   Psalm 139:14
Proverbs 3:7-8   Jeremiah 1:5
Proverbs 4:20-22   Genesis 1:29
1 Corinthians 6:12-13, AMP   Isaiah 44:24
1 Thessalonians 5:23-24

This prayer will help you speak positive words over your health:

Father, in the name of Jesus, Your word says that I was bought with a price, the precious blood of Jesus. I now realize that I owe all to Him. His sacrifice on the cross made my life with you possible. I will value the body that Jesus died for me to have. I will consider His life for me in my choices where I take my body, what I put into my body, and what I put on my body. I will live mindful of my debt to Him, and I will purpose to live a healthy lifestyle. I will learn how to take care of my body with the proper exercise and diet.

Father, you have given us good and healthy food that grows from the ground and healthy meat to sustain ourselves. I will use what you have given me to live long and strong and declare your glory. I will not allow unhealthy food choices to

67

open the door to sickness in my life that will cause me to focus more on myself than on others. I refuse to allow unhealthy choices to shift the focus of my faith to healing rather than sharing the Kingdom's Gospel. I choose to help others live the blessed life that Jesus purchased for them with His blood. You have given me every herb bearing seed, plant, the tree for food to maintain good health.

Father, I will use the self-control that You have given me in the *fruits of the spirit* (Galatians 5:22-24). I will make proper choices that will allow me to fulfill my God-given purpose. *In Jesus' Name, Amen.*

Faith in Action

1. Read Proverbs 7:23. What is the benefit of departing from evil?

2. As a Christian, how come you no longer own your body (1 Corinthians 6:19-20)?

3. What does sin lead to? (Hint: see Romans 5:12)

4. What path does sin use to bring death? (Hint: S_ _ Kn_ _s and D_ Se_ s_.)

5. What type of exercises do you enjoy?

6. What plan have you developed that will lead to healthy, balanced meals?

7. Read 1 Thessalonians 5:23-24. As you see in this verse, your spirit and soul are two different things. What is your soul? (According to Proverbs 2:10 your mind, Job 7:15 your will, Song of Solomon 1:7 your emotions, these three components make up your soul) Through Bible reading, study, and meditation, you will train your soul to align itself with your spirit. Now your spirit and soul can lead your body to live for God.

8. Your soul's prosperity is an integral part of the plan for a healthy lifestyle (3 John 2). What can you do to nurture the maturity of your soul?

9. Read Galatian 5:24 and 1 Corinthians 15:31. What do they mean to you?

10. Create a confession from Galatian 5:24 and 1 Corinthians 15:31.

Chapter 16
Diligence

The Book of Proverbs teaches us that the diligent will rule (be in charge). Laziness will result in the opposite! We should not accept from ourselves what we would not accept from others. For example, your parents tell you they want to go to the mall, but they want the house cleaned first. Suddenly you have all the energy you need to clean quickly and appropriately. However, your parents have a standard of how they want the house kept daily. But you pick and choose when you will do what they request at the level they desire. That is not diligence, but rather rebellion, and the Bible refers to rebellion as the *sin of witchcraft.*

The character trait of diligence means you are a hard worker in all things. You adopt the motto that anything worth doing is worth doing right! Diligence is what God expects *all* the time as it brings Him honor. This principle applies to children of all ages, students, and employees alike. Colossians 3:23-24 states, "Whatever you do, work at it with all your heart, as unto the Lord." Deuteronomy 5:16 states, "honor your mother and father, and it will go well with you." When you are diligent at school, work, home, and neighborhood, you are a witness and testimony for God. Make those who are in authority over you proud of you. Most of all, make God proud!

The following scriptures will help you understand the importance of diligence:

Proverbs 12:24, 27   Deuteronomy 4:9
Proverbs 22:29   Psalm 119:4
Proverbs 19:15   Proverbs 8:17
Exodus 15:26   Hebrews 11:6

This prayer will help you speak diligence over and into your life:

Father, in the name of Jesus, in Your word, You asked me to do everything unto You, not with eye service or lip service as if I am trying to please men. I am to be mindful that my life is meant to please You; therefore, I commit to being a diligent servant of the Most High God. Because I have heard Your Word and I am committed to doing it, because of this, You will view me as a wise man who has built his home upon a rock (a stable place). Because I am diligent, I will be placed in a place of influence where my light can shine for You. Practicing diligence in my life will work together for good for those around me. They will see that I love You God,

72

and I am concerned about fulfilling my purpose in life for You.

Because I am diligent, I will keep Your Word in my heart so that I will not sin against You, and I will prosper. I will purpose to work with the Holy Spirit to respect You and keep Your commandments. Through this, those around me shall be blessed. Father, I decree that I am diligent in my service to You. I thank You, Father, for the reward of the diligent, which is riches, wealth, honor, and long life. *In Jesus' name, Amen.*

Faith in Action

1. Upon studying Matthew 25:14-30, you will understand that God wants your life to be productive. He graciously gives life, talents, and other provisions to us. He expects a return on His investment (like when people put money in a bank, they expect interest). God has given you a lot of things; His love (Romans 5:5), His faith (Romans 12:3), a new life in Christ (2 Corinthians 5:17), etc. How will you use these gifts to add value to your life and the lives of those around you?

2. After reading Hebrews 1:5, what was Enoch's testimony?

3. What do you think about the reward God gave Enoch?

4. Read Proverbs 29:2. What happens when the diligent rule?

5. According to Proverbs 12:27, what is a prized possession?

6. How much does diligence affect you at school and at home?

7. What is the opposite of diligence?

8. How much will your life be impacted by a lack of diligence?

9. Do you know anyone who is not diligent? What are your feelings about this?

Chapter 17

Healed from Mental/Intellectual, and Emotional Disabilities

With the number of rapidly increasing children born with Autism, Asperger's, ADD/ ADHD, and other forms of mental/intellectual along with emotional disabilities, we must use our faith to conquer these and other mental attacks. The devil's plan is to bring disunity to your family and create what can sometimes feel like favoritism (this can bring loneliness to individuals within your family). The devil wants you as a family to be *inward-focused* (giving attention and focus to the disorder's symptoms). However, God wants you to be *upward and outward-focused* by giving your attention and care to Him (1 Peter 5:7). Share His love with those who have not opened their heart to Him 2 Corinthians 5:17). The Bible teaches that every name (including the names of mental/intellectual and emotional disorders) must bow to the Name of Jesus (Philippians 2:8-11). This will require *faith*! The spiritual is more powerful than the natural (2 Kings 6:17).

The following scriptures are God's plan and how to receive healing from mental disabilities:

1 Corinthians 2:16
Isaiah 53:4-5
2 Corinthians 10:4-6
2 Timothy 1:6-7
Philippians 4:6-9

Matthew 2:1-12
2 Timothy 2:20-22
Isaiah 26:3
Revelation 12:10-11

This prayer will help guide you as you trust God for victory over this ailment:

Father, in the Name of Jesus, I agree with the healing You provided for me through the death, burial, and resurrection of Jesus Christ. That healing is for my whole body, including my mind. You have not given me the spirit of fear, You have given me a spirit of power, a spirit of love, and You have given me, and I receive a *sound mind!* Because of that, I will not be afraid of the doctor's diagnosis. I will use the power in the Word of God to shape my beliefs and love You enough to trust you over what I see.

Father, help me not be conformed to this world but be transformed by renewing my mind through Your Word. Holy Spirit, I ask you to strengthen and renew me in my body so I have the strength to fight the good fight of faith. In the name of Jesus, Father, I ask You to replace sadness and depression with joy, defeat with victory, and helplessness with praise, worship, and prayer. During these times, Holy Spirit help me focus on Your love and grace by bringing all things to my memory that concern You, Your love, and Your expected end for my life. Father, You asked me to give my attention to what is good and what is lovely and of an excellent report.

Help me to keep Your commandments and embrace those things in my heart. Father, I will guard my heart and my mind from the fiery darts of the enemy. I will always hear Your voice and obey Your will. Father, I overcome fear with the faith You have given me. Thank you, God, for strengthening my family members and caregivers. Help them always walk in Your peace and love because sometimes it can be challenging.

Father help my parents find a doctor, therapists, and other medical professionals who trust You first. God, I choose to deny theories, ideas, thoughts, and reasonings that do not agree with Your Word. I will lead those thoughts away from my heart, mind, and life and allow Your Word to have first place. In You, Father, I am more than a conqueror. I say that I am healed, set free, delivered, and restored! *In Jesus' Name, Amen.*

Faith in Action

1. Write 2 Timothy 1:6-7, using the following bible versions: New Living Translation (NLT), the Amplified Bible (AMP), and the English Standard Version (ESV).

2. Romans 10: 17 states, "So then faith comes by hearing, and hearing by the Word of God."

3. With faith as your anchor, there is no condition cannot be changed. Read Matthew 19:26. What is impossible for God?

4. You have to use diligence to read, study, and meditate on scripture, so you doubt anything that doesn't agree with the Word of God.

5. Read 2 Corinthians 10:4-6 and create a confession.

6. According to Isaiah 26:3, what will happen in your mind if you keep it on God and His Word?

7. If you put Romans 12:1-2 in practice, what will happen to your mind?

8. According to 1 Corinthians 2:16, what will happen to your mind?

Chapter 18
Evangelism

The Great Commission of *Evangelism*, found in Matthew 28:18-29, states, "And Jesus came and spoke to them, saying, 'All authority has been given to Me in heaven and on earth. Go therefore and make Disciples (people who follow Jesus and his teaching through scripture) of all the nations, baptizing them in the name of the Father and of the Son and of the Holy Spirit, teaching them to observe all things that I have commanded you; and lo, I am with you always, even to the end of the age.' Amen." According to 2 Corinthians 5:18, God has given you the ministry of reconciliation (which is evangelism and will prompt you to pray for individuals to receive Jesus Christ as their Lord and Savior.)

John 3:16 tells us that Jesus died for everyone; this is God's expression of love. Jesus has commanded us to share God's love with *everyone*. The path for anyone you know to become a Disciple, as Jesus has requested, begins with prayer and their experience with you. John 6:44 mentions that people are drawn to God by the Holy Spirit. However, suppose your lifestyle and behavior are not Godly. In that case, non-believers, when they are drawn toward God by the Holy Spirit, may not be interested (1 Peter 2:12). Therefore, we must live honorably in front of everyone. Jesus asked us to lift Him up (by our conversation and lifestyle), so He can draw all men unto Himself. Remember, Jesus died so everyone can have a relationship with God (enemies, friends, family, strangers, teachers, supervisors, people you agree with and people you do not agree with, etc.). God's love is for all!

The following scriptures will assist you in your evangelism efforts:

2 Corinthians 5:18
Romans 15:21
1 Timothy 2:1-4
John 3:3-7

Matthew 28:18-20
1 John 2:1-2
Colossians 2:13
Romans 10:8-10

Use this prayer when praying for someone to open their heart to Jesus:

Father, in the name of Jesus, you commanded (John 3:7) that we be born again. It's Your desire that all men be saved and to come into the knowledge of the truth. Father, I bring _____ before you today, I am praying that they will accept your Son Jesus Christ as their Lord and

Savior. I pray that the troubles in _____ life won't cause them to believe that this is your plan for their life. Holy Spirit help _____ see that their life experiences are not the determination of God's Love. Holy Spirit, help me with my actions and my words so that I can lift Jesus up, so they will be drawn to God and begin their new creation life with you.

Jesus laid down His life for _____. Jesus hung on the cross for _____. Jesus shed His blood for _____ so that he/she can have a relationship with you Father. Jesus became sin for _____ so that he/she can become the righteousness of God in Christ Jesus. Father it is your will all men be saved, and none perish. God you so greatly loved us that you sent your only begotten Son, so that whosoever would believe on Him would have everlasting life I speak everlasting life for_____. *In Jesus' Name, Amen.*

Faith in Action

1. Read Matthew 28:18-20.

2. Write out verses 19-20.

3. What did Jesus command you to go make?

4. Write the definition of that word?

5. According to John 3:16 and 1 John 2:1-2, is there anyone Jesus did not die for?

6. In John 3:5-7, Jesus stated that people must be born of (Hints: W_ _ _ and of the S_ _ _ _ _) to enter the Kingdom of God.

7. Read and study Romans 10:8-10. Name the parts to the Sinner's Prayer? (Hints: Con_ _ _ _, Bel_ _ _ _, then A_k Jesus to be your L_ _d and S_ _ _ _r.)

8. Write the prayer in your own words so that you are to use it when necessary.

Chapter 19

My Neighborhood

We all live in neighborhoods (urban and suburban communities, ghettos, barrios, "the hood," etc.). These become part of our world that affects the rest of our lives. Be friendly to your neighbors, help them when and where you can. Simple things like cutting their lawn, placing their trash can at the curb or putting it away, and shoveling their driveway and sidewalk as well, etc., are characteristics of a good neighbor. Be mindful that Jesus commanded you to *love your neighbor as you love yourself* (Matthew 22:39).

We must let our lights shine (through God-inspired good works) for all men to see (Matthew 5:16). Become the person that your neighbors can turn to in times of trouble, for prayer, help, a hug, or a kind word. Whether the Holy Spirit allows you to discern or when your neighbor verbalizes a problem, be specific by stating aloud their names and issues to God. If you have received the Promise of the Father (Luke 24:49) which is praying in tongues, allow the Holy Spirit to use this heavenly communication method to intercede on behalf of your neighbors. Share the life that God has given you with others!

The following scriptures will demonstrate loving behavior to your neighbor:

Matthew 5:16
James 4:10
John 13:34-35
1 Peter 1:22

Romans 12:9-10
1 John 4:11
Colossians 3:12-13
Philippians 2:1-4

Use this prayer to benefit your neighbors and neighborhood:

Father, in the Name of Jesus, I bring my neighborhood to You today in prayer. My neighborhood is not made of buildings, but rather the people who live here, and that you sent Your son Jesus to die for. God, Your commandment requires me to love them as I love myself. So, I pray for safety, peace, mercy, healing, favor, and the blessing of God for them today. Holy Spirit, show me if there's anything I can do today to help and serve my neighbors.

Father, I pray that my neighbors have an open ear and heart to You today so that they do not miss their day of visitation (when the Holy Spirit tries to help them open their hearts to God). Holy Spirit, give them a heart to know You and draw closer to You. I pray that my neighbors would choose life today, that they would not yield to the ideas or emotions that lead them to unsafe thinking, followed by poor choices. Father, You promised to shine the sun on the just and unjust, so help my neighbors see Your kindness for them today. Holy Spirit, lead my neighbor to someone today who will have a word of encouragement for them or words that lead them closer to a relationship with You. Holy Spirit, help me see my part in my neighbor's salvation.

Father, I am committed to using Your love that You have given me for my neighbor, and I will serve You by serving them and helping them in any way that I can. I will let the light You have placed in me shine to draw them to You. Lord, show yourself strong unto them, mightily pouring out Your Spirit upon them in a manner they cannot resist You. They are Your people, and I believe they will return unto You with all their heart. *In Jesus' Name, Amen.*

Faith in Action

1. Read Colossians 3:10 – 17.

2. What does verse 10 tell you to put on?

3. In verse 11, does one's ethnicity or culture have anything to do with you loving them the same way you love yourself?

4. According to verse 12, what are to put on every day?

5. Verse 13 tells us to do the same thing for others that Jesus did for us. What is it?

6. In order for you to be the kind of neighbor that God desires, what must rule your heart (verse 15). Why is it important that you live as a good neighbor?

7. Who are you serving when you are kind to your neighbor?

8. Verse 17 says, "giving thanks to God," this instructs you to take the opportunity to thank God for helping your neighbor. When they thank you for helping them, here's an example response "No problem, I thank God for the strength to help you." This lets them know that God blessed them through you; the Holy Spirit uses you as a part of His plan to win them to Christ.

9. Luke 10:25-37 tells the story of the Good Samaritan. Please read and write down your thoughts.

Chapter 20

Forgiveness

The most popular scripture in the Bible is John 3:16. This scripture states, "For God so loved the world that He gave His only begotten Son, that whoever believes in Him should not perish but have everlasting life." He gave the keywords, which portrays God as the *giver* He is! He has given us *forgiveness,* the most valuable thing through the life, sacrifice, and the blood of Jesus. At times, the family can need the most forgiveness because of their closeness to you. They can say words that can penetrate our minds and hearts and often build walls that block the growth of the relationship. The effort it takes to love your neighbor (this includes family) as you love yourself the way God commands will require forgiveness.

As humans, we are *not* perfect; we make mistakes and poor choices in our actions and words. There will be times when you will need God's forgiveness. Give that same forgiveness to others when their actions and words affect you. Jesus made it clear that if you don't forgive others, God will not forgive you (Matthew 6:14-15). Therefore, unforgiveness is a <u>**sin**</u>. Since God is willing to forgive anything, your unwillingness to forgive is ***idolatry***, which opposes God. Ephesians 5:1 states we are to imitate God our Father. This means that people should say the same thing about you that they say about God. _____ (insert your name here) forgives people always.

The following scriptures will teach you the importance of forgiving:

Romans 12:9-21   2 Corinthians 2:5-11
Matthew 6:14-15   Ephesians 4:30-32
Luke 17:3   Luke 23:34
Matthew 18:21-23

This prayer will help you walk in forgiveness:

Father, in the name of Jesus, Your love for me and others has no end. You have given us Your best so that forgiveness is available for the entire world. I will not participate with the devil by holding someone in a place of unforgiveness. Through the life-sacrifice, death, burial, and resurrection of Jesus the Christ, our Messiah, you have already made a way of escape. Holy Spirit, please help me to not become a prisoner to unforgiveness. Jesus, You told me that offenses would come in this life. I will activate the ***fruit [no "s"] of the spirit*** in my life so that I will live honorable before

You. I speak gentleness, mercifulness, and the willingness to forgive into my life.

Father, Your love is in my heart for times like this when someone has hurt me. I will use it to remember that the person who hurt me needs Your love now just as much as I do. I forgive willful and accidental trespasses from others. God, I ask You to heal me now and heal the other person who has hurt me today. Father, I ask for Your forgiveness if I have provoked the actions that someone did to me. Holy Spirit, help me be kind and tenderhearted to the person who has hurt me as You have requested (with the same love Jesus showed to Judas). Jesus sacrificed for me, and love does not keep the account of a suffered wrong. Therefore, I will sacrifice the hurt from this offense. Again, Father, I thank You for healing the person who hurt me, as I receive Your healing also. Father, I forgive _____, Lord bless, heal, and love them into right relationship with You. *In Jesus' Name, Amen.*

Faith in Action

1. Have you chosen to give your life to God through Jesus Christ, the Messiah who shed His blood on the cross for you?

2. You must remember that Jesus died for the person who has done something wrong to you. Since God is willing to forgive their sin, you can NOT place yourself higher than Him. Not forgiving someone as a Christian is like going to jail for someone else's crime. You wouldn't do that, would you?

3. Is there anyone that you need to forgive? If so, please repent to God for not managing your emotions and then say, out loud, I forgive _____ (enter person's name).

4. Forgiveness is an act of (Hint: l_ v_).

5. Forgiving someone shows them God's (Hint: l_ v_).

6. Is forgiveness an emotion?

7. Forgiveness is done by (Hint: Fa_ _h).

8. Does someone need to ask for your forgiveness for you to forgive them?

9. Read Ephesians 4:28-32. How will this help you forgive someone?

10. ***Point of information.*** When people, especially those related to you mistreat you, and do not apologize, they may not value the relationship. This can be the result of failing to manage their emotions. However, discipleship requires that you make the right choice and ***forgive!***

Chapter 21

Preparation for Ministry: The Father's Promise

Jesus walked with the disciples for 3.5 years, and they had struggles that were rooted in unbelief and doubt. Their inability to accept everything that Jesus told them was caused by the past's mental trap. The message that the Messiah was coming had been passed down since Moses's death. Be mindful that 400 years had passed from the Old Testament to the New Testament. So, when Jesus shows up, the Jewish people in that time still had their challenges with the Roman government. They hoped that Jesus would come with a *sword* (meaning they wanted Him to show up with a massive army, angels, weapons, etc.) and take over. But remember Jesus is the Word of God made flesh, the Word comes to bring faith. So, He came to establish faith in His Disciples and the Israelite's hearts. While they had flashes and periods of faith, they were inconsistent.

After Jesus fulfills His purpose of sacrificing His life on the Cross and is raised up in three days like He promised, they believed totally. But what was Jesus' response? Was He elated? Did He ordain them and send them out to spread the Gospel of the Kingdom? No! This was His response, according to Luke 24. Instead, He opened up their understanding, imparting supernatural information regarding Himself and their purpose. He explained that He (Luke 24:49) was sending the Father's Promise. They were to *tarry or wait* in Jerusalem until they have received the Promise of the Father (power from on high). The Promise of the Father is the *Holy Spirit*.

Moreover, He stated that the Holy Spirit is the third person in the triune God (the Father, Son, and Holy Spirit). The Holy Spirit is equal with God and Jesus. We engage with the Holy Spirit daily as we work out our salvation with fear and trembling (Philippians 2:12).

So, the disciples followed Jesus' instructions and tarried in Jerusalem. In the Upper Room, according to Acts 1, they gathered, including Mary, the mother of Jesus. Furthermore, Acts 1 recounts how the Holy Spirit came in as the sound of a rushing, mighty wind. This miraculous event culminated in them speaking other tongues as the Holy Spirit gave them utterance. He gives you the words, but you must open your mouth and speak them. So, the Disciples had the

Bible evidence of speaking in other tongues, which added to their ministry effectiveness. Paul said, "I thank my God, I speak in tongues more than you all (1 Corinthians 14:18). This statement shows you the emphasis that Paul places on the necessity of taking full advantage of the Father's Promise, which includes praying in tongues (in the Spirit).

5 Reasons to Speak in Tongues

1. Praying in tongues allows you to pray the perfect will of God for you and others without demonic interference (Romans 8:28-27).

2. Praying in tongues allows you to pray the perfect will of God for you and others without demonic interference (Romans 8:28-27).

3. Praying in tongues builds you up spiritually (1 Corinthians 14: 4, Jude 1:20).

4. Praying in tongues allows you to give heartfelt thanks and praise to God for what He has done and wants to do in and through your life (1 Corinthians 14:15-17).

5. Praying in tongues yields your tongue to God for His benefit (James 3:8).

6. Praying in tongues keeps you conscious of the Holy Spirit (John 14:16-17).

Therefore, since Jesus demanded that the Disciples, He spent 3.5 years **not** go forth to fulfill His commandment of making disciples **without** the Holy Spirit, this applies to us ALL!

The following scriptures will give you the basis for the receiving the Promise of the Father:

John 14:16-17   Ephesians 6:10-18
1 Corinthians 14:2-15, 18, 27   Jude 1:20
Acts 1 & 2   Luke 24:36-50

This prayer will direct you as you seek and receive the Promise of the Father:

Father in Heaven, through the shed Blood of Jesus, I have access to you. I have asked and received Jesus as my Savior and Lord. Today I choose to follow His command of receiving the Promise of the Father. Jesus said, if I asked you for bread, you wouldn't give me a serpent. He said if I believe in Him as the scriptures say, rivers of living water will flow from me. I realize I need the overflowing presence of the Holy Spirit so I can live to honor You. Father, I ask You now to fill me with Your Promise in the name of Jesus. I yield myself to the fullness and the power that is the Holy Spirit. I am a *born-again, Spirit-filled Christian*. I yield my tongue to the utterance of the Holy Spirit. I will speak in other tongues and glorify my Father in Heaven. [Now take a breath and release His Power!] *In Jesus' Name, Amen.*

Faith in Action

1. What did Jesus ask His disciples to do once they said they totally believed in Him [Luke 24:49]

2. What city did Jesus want them to assemble in [Acts 1:4]

3. What did Jesus say the disciple and the others assembled would be Baptized with? [Acts 1:5]

4. What did Jesus say they would receive in Acts 1:8?

5. And once the received p_____, what would they become? W_____s

6. Read Acts 2:1-4 in the Amplified Version of the Bible.

7. Does the Holy Spirit speak for you when you are praying in tongues [vs 4]

8. When the Holy Spirit came in verse 2 it was similar to a r_____ m_____ w___.

Chapter 22
The Sinner's Prayer

God, today, I now realize just how much You love me, and I thank You so much for that. Your word tells me that if I believe in my heart that You sent Jesus to die on the cross for me and that You raised Him from the dead for me, then I can confess Him as my Lord and Savior. I believe!

Today _____,_____20___, I ask You God to forgive my sins, and I ask Jesus to be my Lord and Savior.

Thank You, God, for Your forgiveness and for welcoming me into the **Body of Christ**. Jesus, in You, I am a new creation. I surrender my life to You, and I now choose to pursue the life and purpose You have for me. ***In Jesus' Name, Amen.***

Additional Resources
- The Proverbs 22:6 Plan -

The following examples will help you empower your child:

1. **Lead them to welcome Jesus into their heart.**

   Explain God's expansive plan for them and how much He wants to have a relationship with them.

2. **Teach them to praise God.**

   Thanking God and appreciating God for all He is displays our love for Him.

3. **Teach them to have joy.**

   Nehemiah 8:10, "The joy of the Lord is your strength." Joy is not based on situations; it's more about eternal (having a relationship with God), joy than natural (based on circumstances in your life) joy.

4. **Empower them to pray.**

   The necessity of prayer was modeled by Jesus. He got up early and sometimes stayed up all night praying.

5. **Empower them to develop a relationship with the Holy Spirit.**

   Luke 24:49 refers to The Holy Spirit as the ***Promise of the Father***. The Holy Spirit will be with them every day to help them grow in godliness.

6. **Teach them how to recognize satan.**

   Satan is not living on earth dressed in red with horns and a pitchfork. Satan often gets you to give in to negative emotions (hate, lying, disrespectful behavior, etc.).

7. **Teach them obedience.**

   Being obedient to authority (parents, other older family members, teachers, civil servants, etc.). Following God's Word and the Holy Spirit will lead them to be successful in God's eyes.

8. **Teach them the value of keeping their word.**

   Being a person of honor and not being perceived as dishonest will be valuable in relationship building.

9. **Teach them to be diligent.**

   Putting forth the necessary effort to accomplish tasks, chores, schoolwork, sports, etc., will prevent them from having regrets.

10. **Train them to honor their dreams.**

    While every dream is not from God, He often speaks to us in dreams (Peter, Joseph. etc.). Dreams will also help them to expand their thinking beyond their ability. There are *no* great men, there are only great dreams. When you accomplish your dreams often people view you as a great man.

- Prayers from The Bible -

Prayer for Spiritual Strength (Ephesians 3:14-21)

[14] For this reason I bow my knees to the Father [a]of our Lord Jesus Christ, [15] from whom the whole family in heaven and earth is named, [16] that He would grant you, according to the riches of His glory, to be strengthened with might through His Spirit in the inner man, [17] that Christ may dwell in your hearts through faith; that you, being rooted and grounded in love, [18] may be able to comprehend with all the saints what *is* the width and length and depth and height— [19] to know the love of Christ which passes knowledge; that you may be filled with all the fullness of God. [20] Now to Him who is able to do exceedingly abundantly above all that we ask or think, according to the power that works in us, [21] to Him *be* glory in the church by Christ Jesus to all generations, forever and ever. Amen.

Prayer for Spiritual Wisdom (Ephesians 1:15-23)

[15] Therefore I also, after I heard of your faith in the Lord Jesus and your love for all the saints, [16] do not cease to give thanks for you, making mention of you in my prayers: [17] that the God of our Lord Jesus Christ, the Father of glory, may give to you the spirit of wisdom and revelation in the knowledge of Him, [18] the eyes of your [a]understanding being enlightened; that you may know what is the hope of His calling, what are the riches of the glory of His inheritance in the saints, [19] and what *is* the exceeding greatness of His power toward us who believe, according to the working of His mighty power [20] which He worked in Christ when He raised Him from the dead and seated *Him* at His right hand in the

heavenly *places,* ²¹ far above all principality ⁽ᵇ⁾ and ⁽ᶜ⁾power and ⁽ᵈ⁾might and dominion, and every name that is named, not only in this age but also in that which is to come. ²² And He put all *things* under His feet and gave Him *to be* head over all *things* to the church, ²³ which is His body, the fullness of Him who fills all in all.

Paul's Prayer for those supporting him in ministry
(Philippians 1:3-11)

³ I thank my God upon every remembrance of you, ⁴ always in every prayer of mine making request for you all with joy, ⁵ for your fellowship in the gospel from the first day until now, ⁶ being confident of this very thing, that He who has begun a good work in you will complete *it* until the day of Jesus Christ; ⁷ just as it is right for me to think this of you all, because I have you in my heart, inasmuch as both in my chains and in the defense and confirmation of the gospel, you all are partakers with me of grace. ⁸ For God is my witness, how greatly I long for you all with the affection of Jesus Christ. ⁹ And this I pray, that your love may abound still more and more in knowledge and all discernment, ¹⁰ that you may approve the things that are excellent, that you may be sincere and without offense till the day of Christ, ¹¹ being filled with the fruits of righteousness which *are* by Jesus Christ, to the glory and praise of God.

The Lord's Prayer *(Matthew 6:9-13)*

⁹ In this manner, therefore, pray: Our Father in heaven, Hallowed be your name. ¹⁰ Your kingdom come. Your will be done on earth as *it is* in heaven. ¹¹ Give us this day our daily bread. ¹² And forgive us our debts, as we

forgive our debtors. [13] And do not lead us into temptation but deliver us from the evil one. For yours is the kingdom and the power and the glory forever. Amen.

Aaron Blessing *(Numbers 6:24-26)*

[24] The Lord bless you and keep you; [25] The Lord make His face shine upon you, and be gracious to you; [26] The Lord lift up His countenance upon you, and give you peace.

A Prayer for Deliverance and Forgiveness *(Psalm 25:1-6)*

[1] To you, O Lord, I lift up my soul. [2] O my God, I trust in you; let me not be ashamed; let not my enemies triumph over me. [3] Indeed, let no one who waits on You be ashamed; let those be ashamed who deal treacherously without cause. [4] Show me Your ways, O Lord; teach me Your paths. [5] Lead me in Your truth and teach me, for you *are* the God of my salvation; on You I wait all the day. [6] Remember, O Lord, Your tender mercies, and Your loving kindnesses, for they *are* from of old.

The Prayer of Jabez *(1 Chronicles 4:10)*

[10]And Jabez called on the God of Israel saying, "Oh, that You would bless me indeed, and enlarge my territory, that Your hand would be with me, and that You would keep *me* from evil, that I may not cause pain!" So, God granted him what he requested.

THE *Praying* CHILD

Jesus Prays for Himself (John 17:1-5)

[17] Jesus spoke these words, lifted up His eyes to heaven, and said: "Father, the hour has come. Glorify Your Son, that your Son also may glorify You, [2] as you have given Him authority over all flesh, that He should give eternal life to as many as You have given Him. [3] And this is eternal life, that they may know You, the only true God, and Jesus Christ whom You have sent. [4] I have glorified You on the earth. I have finished the work which You have given me to do. [5] And now, O Father, glorify me together with Yourself, with the glory which I had with You before the world was.

Jesus Prays for His Disciples (John 17:6-19)

[6] I have manifested your name to the men whom you have given me out of the world. They were yours, you gave them to me, and they have kept your word. [7] Now they have known that all things which you have given me are from you. [8] For I have given to them the words which you have given me; and they have received *them,* and have known surely that I came forth from you; and they have believed that you sent me. [9] I pray for them. I do not pray for the world but for those whom you have given me, for they are yours. [10] And all Mine are yours, and yours are Mine, and I am glorified in them. [11] Now I am no longer in the world, but these are in the world, and I come to you. Holy Father, keep through your name those whom you have given me, that they may be one as We *are.* [12] While I was with them in the world, I kept them in your name. Those whom you gave me I have kept; and none of them is lost except the son of perdition, that the Scripture might be fulfilled. [13] But now I come to you, and these things I speak in the world, that they may have My joy fulfilled in themselves.

[14] I have given them your word; and the world has hated them because they are not of the world, just as I am not of the world. [15] I do not pray that you should take them out of the world, but that you should keep them from the evil one. [16] They are not of the world, just as I am not of the world. [17] Sanctify them by your truth. Your word is truth. [18]As you sent me into the world, I also have sent them into the world. [19]And for their sakes I sanctify Myself, that they also may be sanctified by the truth.

Jesus Prays for All Believers (John 17:20-26)

[20] I do not pray for these alone, but also for those who will believe in me through their word; [21] that they all may be one, as you, Father, *are* in me, and I in you; that they also may be one in Us, that the world may believe that you sent me. [22] And the glory which you gave me I have given them, that they may be one just as We are one: [23] I in them, and you in me; that they may be made perfect in one, and that the world may know that you have sent me and have loved them as you have loved me. [24]Father, I desire that they also whom you gave me may be with me where I am, that they may behold My glory which you have given me; for you loved me before the foundation of the world. [25] O righteous Father! The world has not known you, but I have known you; and these have known that you sent me. [26] And I have declared to them your name, and will declare *it,* that the love with which you loved me may be in them, and I in them.

Daily Confessions from The Ten Commandments

ONE:

You are the Lord, my God. I will have no other gods before You, not myself or any other person, not my feelings or desires; therefore, I will have Your favor.

TWO:

I will not use the Lord's name negatively or in profane speaking. I will use His name in prayer for people He sent Jesus to die for.

THREE:

"I was glad when they said, let us go into the house of the Lord!" I will honor the Lord's day by attending church consistently.

FOUR:

I will honor my father and mother by following their instructions, teachings and giving them honor and respect as the God-given authority in my life.
My parents are a blessing in my life.

FIVE:

Life is very valuable to God, that is why He sent His Son Jesus to die for all of us. I will take no one's life ever! I will share the Gospel of the Kingdom with people to bring them into the Eternal and Blessed life that God desires for them. Everyone deserves the love of God!

SIX:

My spiritual growth in God is *very* important to me. I will pursue my God-given purpose. God has begun a good work in me, and I will work with the Holy Spirit, so I can do great things for God.

SEVEN:

I will not steal! Stealing is me providing for myself. God loves me, and He provides for my needs; therefore, I *refuse* to steal.

EIGHT:

I will not lie! I am honest. My mouth is available for God, I will use His words for prayer and encourage others.

NINE:

God has given me a loving family; I will honor God by loving my family as God does.

TEN:

I will not be jealous or envious of others. God gives me what I need, and He is looking for ways to give me more from the abundance He has already provided for me.

An Outline of Prayer
(Matthew 6:9-13)

Prayer is *two-way* communication with God. What prayer is NOT is us, His children, entering a *one-way* communication where we tell God what we feel or need Him to do for us. Taking our daily concerns to God is what He requires (1 Peter 5:7); however, and more importantly, is the fact that He desires to spend time with us, and He wants to say something to us. He also has requests for our day and life. Imagine how you would feel if someone came to you repeatedly, tells you what they want you to do, then walks away and might say thank you. This reflects, for many Believers, what prayer looks like. Listed below is a brief explanation for prayer's multi-facets: worship, praise, quietness, repentance and humility, direction, daily concerns/cares, and thanksgiving.

- *Worship God:* Talk to God about who He is. This helps you exalt and keep Him in His proper place.

- *Praise God:* Be thankful to Him because He has your life in His hands.

- *Quietness:* Settle yourself to hear His voice or sense His presence to direct you.

- *Repentance & Humility:* Apologize to God for the times you are not looking, talking, or acting like Him in word, deed, or attitude. Let Him know that you are relying on Him.

- *Direction:* Yield (your day, time, and energy) and talk to the Holy Spirit, ask Him to lead you today, and commit to serving Him today.

- *Daily Concerns/Cares:* For you, your loved ones, or anyone in your sphere of influence (neighbors, students, co-workers).

- *Thanksgiving:* Thank God for hearing and answering your prayers (1 John 5: 14-15, KJV).

Listening to music while praying is an excellent addition to your time alone with The Lord! Included at the end of this book are pages that you can use as a prayer journal to record your prayers and God's answers to you.

THE *Praying* CHILD

My Prayer Journal

Page 1

REQUEST DATE:	TOPIC(S):	ANSWERED DATE:

GOD'S PROMISE FROM SCRIPTURE CONCERNING MY REQUEST: (BIBLE BOOK, CHAPTER(S), VERSE(S)

MY REQUEST:

GOD'S ANSWER TO ME:

My Prayer Journal

REQUEST DATE:	TOPIC(S):	ANSWERED DATE:

MY REQUEST (CONTINUED):

GOD'S ANSWER TO ME (CONTINUED):

About the Authors

Elder Norman C. Jones

Elder Norman C. Jones began his journey walking with God in November 1995 while living in Detroit, MI attending Word of Faith Christian Center. Elder Jones returned to Philadelphia in the Spring of 1996, where he continued attending Word of Faith-Phila (one of the many satellite churches worldwide). Elder Jones met his wife soon after returning; they wed in August of 1998. Elder Jones served in the Ministry of Helps there and in the Summer of 2001 was asked to join the Deacon's Ministry. Elder Jones was ordained as a Deacon in October 2001. Elder Jones began attending Rhema Correspondence Bible School in 2000.

In the Fall of 2000, WOFCC-Philadelphia began Laymen's Bible School, a two-year program; Elder Jones was a part of the first graduating class in May of 2002. Elder Jones has consistently participated in spreading the Good News of the Kingdom of God, including street witnessing, nursing home, shelter, prison, and individual discipleship. Elder Jones graduated from the Melvin Floyd School of Evangelism in May of 2013. In 2008 the call to ministry led Elder Jones to move on from WOFCC-Philadelphia and join Freedom

Christian Bible Fellowship-Norristown. He rejoined Pastors Darin C. and Stephanie Park, whom he served with in Youth Ministry at WOFCC-Philadelphia. Elder Jones was ordained in November 2009.

In November 2010, Freedom Norristown became Living Water Outreach Worship Center (which is now Living Water Discipleship Ministries), where he has continued to serve. Elder Jones is a teacher of God's Word and is excited to participate in disciples' spiritual growth. Elder Jones' messages promote Christlikeness, along with the individual fulfillment of God's purpose. Elder Jones was ordained as an Elder and elevated to Assistant Pastor of Living Water Outreach Worship Center (which is now Living Water Discipleship Ministries) in Norristown, Pennsylvania, in November of 2018.

Elder Shelley Jones

Shelley received the Lord at the age of 10 years old. As she went to her aunt's Christian camp in Macon, Georgia, throughout her early years; this was when the Lord spoke to her heart (Revelations 3:20). In 1992, Shelley rededicated her life to the Lord and has been growing as a disciple ever since. She joined the Word of Faith Christian Center in Philadelphia, where she learned Biblical truths under Pastor Keith Echols. street witnessing, discipleship, children's church, choir, outreach ministry, and youth camp counselor were places where she served in the ministry.

In the Fall of 2000, WOFCC-Philadelphia began Laymen's Bible School, a two-year program. Shelley Jones was a part of the first graduating class in May of 2002. Her heart has always been to work with children. She and her husband Norman were prompted by God to work and reside at Christ's Home for Children in Pennsylvania. Hired as House Parents, they took care of children in need for 5 years.

In 2008 the Shelley was called to serve under Pastors Darin C. and Stephanie Park at Living Water Outreach Worship Center (which is now Living Water Discipleship Ministries) in Norristown, Pennsylvania. There she was licensed in October 2015 as a Minister at Living Waters. Also, in 2018 Shelley became an ordained Elder of Living Waters, where she continues to serve.

Shelley has consistently participated in spreading the Good News of the Kingdom of God. Her activities include street witnessing, visitation at nursing homes, shelters, prisons, and group home for women who have been victimized. She also participates in a discipleship program, which she loves. Shelley's background also includes working for the Norristown School District's Special Education Department children. Her interest and commitment to working with special needs children extended to Access Services in Fort Washington, Pennsylvania. She continues to teach the Good News of the Gospel, helping disciples grow in the Lord, reaching those who are hurting, and helping people who need love and kindness.

CPSIA information can be obtained
at www.ICGtesting.com
Printed in the USA
BVHW041341300621
610774BV00006B/31

9 781942 871965